Deep Mysteries
of the
BLOOD

with

Prophetic Prayers to Combat
Blood-Related Spiritual War

Updated Edition

by

Ebenezer Gabriels & Abigail Ebenezer-Gabriels

© Ebenezer Gabriels Publishing
First Published - March 2020
Updated - October 2021
ISBN 9781950579983

Ebenezer Gabriels Ministries Mailing
19644 Club House Road Suite 815
Gaithersburg, Maryland 20886

www.EbenezerGabriels.Org
hello@ebenezergabriels.org

DEDICATION

To the Father who loved us so much to sacrifice the Lamb, the only Son of God who for the sins of those who were undeserving of such love.

We worship you by the blood of the Lamb.

Let the blood of the Lamb make whole every broken life reading this book, and let the power in the blood of the Lamb be revealed to all through this book.

In Jesus Name, Amen.

CONTENT

ABOUT DEEPER MYSTERIES OF THE BLOOD

The lasting impact of the life, death and resurrection of Jesus is displayed by the power in the blood of Jesus. Life primarily resides in the blood, and many spiritual problems dwell in the blood. The study of the blood is mandatory for any believer who will command the authority of the blood of Jesus. In the book, *Deep Mysteries of the Blood*, Prophet Ebenezer Gabriels and Pastor Abigail Ebenezer Gabriels share revelation on the secrets of the blood, the enemy's uses of the blood, types of battles within the blood and how to confront wars originating from the blood. This book opens up new revelations on the understanding of the blood, arms readers with the spiritual insights needed to conquer blood-related spiritual warfare and bring believers into a place of profound gratitude for the blood of Jesus.

1

~

A CONFESSION

In one of the most shocking revelations in ministry; it was 2019, and a Sabbath Prophetic Worship Encounter was ongoing, and the Lord opened up a revelation and said to me, *"Decree my Word"*. The Word was specific and it was for a very young lady. Sister, the Lord is saying to you *"You must do away from the association of witchcraft in your network"*. The sister said she goes to certain websites online to read about witchcraft. Worship was over and she was over, and she said she needed to talk. She said, "I am an active witch, a very active one, and I do blood rituals and all that stuff". Then she opened up on some of the hidden mysteries in plain sight and how the enemy transacts using people's blood.

Inquiries about the Enemy's Use of Blood: Demon of Rage

At this time, the Lord began to lead us to ask questions and there were shocking revelations especially because this was a very young lady. We asked, "What do you use blood for?" She said blood is the only currency for making payments to the devil. At first, we were thinking ..how was she getting blood and not getting caught. She said she had the spiritual powers to transfer demons of rage and violence into people. She did this in schools, and when she did that, students who were under her spell would break out in a fight. The fight will get worse, until blood is spilled.   Once the blood is spilled, her blood sacrifice is completed. What this means is that some percentage of the blood spills and bloodshed is as a result of demonic possession, and the devil needing to draw blood. His agents - witches, wizards and other types of agents will use any tactic, like violence, to draw blood to satisfy the requirement of satan.

Inquiries about the Enemy's Use of Blood: A Need for Payment

The lady was in her early 20s. She seemed knowledgeable about what she was talking about. But at first, I thought, maybe she is out of her mind, the Lord said, "she is telling you exactly how things are wrong in their kingdom ". She said anytime she goes against the will of Satan she must repay with blood, hence she needs to find the blood of a human for that payment. This lady says that Satan specifically chooses to use many of her friend's blood whenever she got into trouble. Her friends begin to encounter blood loss, through illnesses, auto accidents and all sorts of mysterious situations, to make repayments to the devil. These friends had no idea of what was happening. She said at some point she became pregnant, and she had no blood to give to the devil, she had to give the blood of the baby in her womb, and the next day, the transaction came as a miscarriage that landed her at the hospital. This confession was the confession of a lady who was just a little over 20 years old. Many illnesses, accidents, loss of pregnancy are not natural and are transactions of darkness upon those lives where they occur.

This confession gave a deeper meaning to the Scripture:

They shed innocent *blood*, the *blood* of their sons and daughters, whom they sacrificed to the idols of Canaan, and the land was desecrated by their *blood*.

Psalm 106:38 NIV

and a related Scripture in the book of Isaiah:

Their feet run to evil,

And they make haste to shed innocent blood....

Isaiah 59:7 NKJV

After this ministry, the Lord said, "this was to show that the children of darkness are very knowledgeable about the use of blood. Workers of iniquity know a lot about the blood, they know how to use the blood for evil, they know how to manipulate through the blood, they know how to shed blood and how to ruin people's lives by blood. This is called the bloody spiritual war".

God wants His children to become equipped with the knowledge of the blood, and most especially, about the powers, the use and the mighty privileges in the BLOOD OF THE LAMB, that was shed for the remissions of our sins, shattering all the walls that separate us from the Father. In this book, we share revelations of the blood we have received from the Father, and we pray that the realities of the blood of Jesus will be yours and your life will be under the absolute management of the blood of Jesus.

PRAYERS FOR REVELATION & PROTECTION OF THE BLOOD FROM DARKNESS

1. Father, thank you for opening up my eyes to understand your Word on this subject of the blood in the name of Jesus.

2. Lord, let the revelation of my bloodline be revealed unto me in the name of Jesus

3. Father, release unto me the knowledge I need for my blood to be protected from the powers of wickedness in the name of Jesus.

4. My blood is under the management of the blood of Jesus.

5. My blood, hear the word of God and live in the name of Jesus.

6. My blood, you are under the management of the Word of life in the name of Jesus

7. My blood, you are under the management of the voice of the Lord.

8. My life will not enter into struggles in the name of Jesus

9. Life will not be snuffed out of my blood in the name of Jesus.

10. Struggles arising from my time in the blood, I am no longer under your yoke in the name of Jesus

11. My blood is not available for satanic activities in the name of Jesus.

12. My blood rejects all forms of manipulation in the name of Jesus.

13. My blood, you are not available for satanic use in the name of Jesus

14. My blood receives the power in the blood of Jesus.

15. Let my blood receive the fresh fire of the Holy Spirit in the name of Jesus.

16. My blood is charged with the fire of God for protection.

17. My blood is charged with the Word of the Lord, in the name of Jesus.

18. My blood is charged with the Spirit of power, in the name of Jesus.

19. My blood is charged with the strength of God in the name of Jesus.

20. My blood is charged with the breath of God in the name of Jesus

NOTES

2

~

WONDERS IN THE BLOOD

Many of the wonders of God reside in the blood. Life resides in the blood, also the power of God resides in the blood. The Scripture notes that the blood is one of the wonders of God, alongside fire, smoke, sun and moon. These creations are ministers of God, ordained to work alongside man while man lives. The Scripture below in the book of Joel testifies of these wonders of God.

"And I will show wonders in the heavens and in the earth:
Blood and fire and pillars of smoke.
The sun shall be turned into darkness,
And the moon into blood,
Before the coming of the great and awesome day of the

Lord.

And it shall come to pass

Joel 2:30-32 NKJV

In the Scripture above, God declared His wonders and classified blood alongside elements such as fire and smoke. In the same discussion, the Lord also mentions the sun and the moon, and strangely says that the moon will be turned into blood before the coming of the Lord. There is a deeper relationship between the blood and the moon that is yet to be uncovered. Spiritually, the elements such as the earth, moon, sun, star, and heaven relate with the blood fluently.

The Ordinance Between the Blood and the Earth

Man has dominion of everything on earth as commanded by God in Genesis 2:24. The moment man sins, and especially blood related sins; abortion, violence, murder which sins spills blood on the earth, the earth becomes defiled and no longer respects the covenant of dominion upon that man. Defilement of the earth takes place whenever blood is shed on the earth as stated in the Scripture below:

"So you shall not pollute the land where you *are;* for blood defiles the land, and no atonement can be made for the land, for the blood that is shed on it, except by the blood of him who shed it"

Numbers 35:33 NKJV

Whenever people shed blood through any form of blood shedding sin, their earth is polluted and the land begins to seek vengeance. The mandate of vengeance is so critical that the land refuses to wipe off the record of iniquity and continues to rage until an atonement is completed.

The Earth Identifies People by Blood

The only way the earth distinguishes everyone is by the blood in them. Job lamented in the book of Job 16:18: " "O earth, do not cover my blood, And let my cry have no *resting* place". The earth identifies each person by blood, and this was why Job instructed the earth concerning his blood. We see this concept today in science where everyone's blood has unique components which are used to identify person A as a different life from person B. Spiritually, the earth identifies humans by their blood and this is why the earth cannot curse person B when Person A is the sinner who sinned on the earth. The earth identifies each of us by our blood. Hence when people commit sins on the earth, and especially blood-related sins, the earth curses and fights against their blood.

Powers of the Sun and Moon over the Blood

Basic science taught us that life is not impossible without the sun. Without the sun, plants will die, animals and humans will also die. This mystery is revealed in the Word of God. In the verse requoted in the book of Joel below;

"And I will show wonders in the heavens and in the earth:
Blood and fire and pillars of smoke.
The sun shall be turned into darkness,
And the moon into blood,
Before the coming of the great and awesome day of the

Lord.

And it shall come to pass

Joel 2:30-32 NKJV

The Scripture says, "And the moon into blood". The sun and the moon especially have powers of life in them. During creation of the earth as captured in Genesis 1, God made the sun to be a source of life, and it was necessary for the sun and moon to be created first before life was formed in man, because the sun provides light, heat and energy needed for the survival of life on earth. Hence if there is no sun, life cannot be sustained on earth.

The sun and the moon are so powerful, that in the spiritual realm, these elements can project diseases into the blood of people. This spiritual technology is often used by workers of iniquity in their various institutions to project infirmities into the blood of people. However, christians who have this revelation of God can work under the covenant in the word which says, "The sun shall not strike you by day, Nor the moon by night"(Psalm 121:6).

The Scripture below speaks concerning the implications

of the sun rising on a thief:

"If a man steals an ox or a sheep, and slaughters it or sells it, he shall restore five oxen for an ox and four sheep for a sheep. If the thief is found breaking in, and he is struck so that he dies, *there shall be* no guilt for his bloodshed. If the sun has risen on him, *there shall be* guilt for his bloodshed. He should make full restitution; if he has nothing, then he shall be sold for his theft.

Exodus 22: 1-3 NKJV

From the Scripture above, we learn that when the sun rises on a thief, there shall be guilt for bloodshed, and a restitution is required. As the sun and moon are witnesses to good things as written in Psalms 89:36-37 - "His seed shall endure forever, And his throne as the sun before Me;It shall be established forever like the moon, Even *like* the faithful witness in the sky, so they bear witnesses against transgressors". The blood does not work in isolation, the blood works with other elements. This is the reason why every covenant the Lord enact with families is kept in the blood, with sun, moon and other elements being witnesses. One of the most powerful covenants made with David called upon the covenants with night and day, by extension, sun and moon as witnesses. The elements are always witnesses to some covenants of God made with man. Covenants of sovereignty, leaders are witnessed by these elements.

"Thus says the Lord: 'If you can break My covenant with the day and My covenant with the night, so that there will not be day and night in their season, then My covenant may also be broken with David My servant, so that he shall not have a son to reign on his throne, and with the Levites, the priests, My ministers"

Jeremiah 33:20-22 NKJV

Such covenants hold that, as long as the sun rules by the day and moon by night, David and his descendants will always be on the throne. Satanists who have access to these secrets sometimes use cunning ways to lure people who carry this covenant to sin against God, and utter utterances into the Sun and Moon, bringing them as witnesses against the sinner, just to give strong reasons to annul covenants of greatness written concerning a man.

The Ordinance of Blood and Life

We discussed that life resides in the blood. Also, a human is a soul and a spirit living in a body. There is also the component of blood that makes us human. The Scripture says the life of the animal is in the blood. The breath of God supplies us with life, and that life is found in the blood. God gave Moses the revelation of the creation. This Scripture mentions that the breath of God carries ife which when breathed into us, gives us life. There is another revelation the Lord showed Moses which reveals the site where life is situated in man. The Scripture below reveals this:

for it is *the life of* all flesh. Its blood sustains its *life*. Therefore I said to *the* children *of* Israel, 'You shall not eat *the* blood *of* any flesh, for *the life of* all flesh is its blood. Whoever eats it shall be cut off.'

Leviticus 17:14 (NKJV)

Because life resides in the blood, blood-related diseases are usually difficult to resolve, and when people lose so much blood, they can die. Also, this is why there is no medical procedure that doctors can guarantee a 100% outcome of success. Whenever blood is involved, doctors speak to patients about risks and chances involved, and leave room for "chances". The chance is a display of absoluteness of God's power, and the unsearchable wisdom of God that has positioned the life of every man inside the blood.

Prophet Ezekiel was given the revelation that God's Word gives life to the blood. See Scripture below:

Ezekiel 16:2-6 (NKJV)

"Son of man, cause Jerusalem to know her abominations, and say, 'Thus says the Lord God to Jerusalem: "Your birth and your nativity *are* from the land of Canaan; your father *was* an Amorite and your mother a Hittite. *As for* your nativity, on the day you were born your navel cord was not cut, nor were you washed in water to cleanse *you;* you were not rubbed with salt nor wrapped in swaddling cloths. No eye pitied you, to do any of these things for you, to have compassion on you; but you

were thrown out into the open field, when you yourself were
loathed on the day you were born. "And when I passed by you
and saw you struggling in your own blood, I said to you in
your blood, 'Live!' Yes, I said to you in your blood, 'Live!'I
made you thrive like a plant in the field; and you grew,
matured, and became very beautiful.

The Ordinance of the Blood and the First Breath

Breathing is a sign of the existence of life and begins after
birth. When a baby is being born, it does not come breathing
from inside the mother's womb. Babies begin breathing after
they have been born. Where there is no breath, it means there is
no life. A study found:

"Around 85% of babies born at term initiate spontaneous
respiration within 10 to 30 s of birth, an additional 10%
require initial steps such as tactile stimulation or airway
clearing or positioning and approximately 3% require
positive-pressure ventilation by bag and mask" (Patel et al

2019)

Breathing begins only after 10 to 30 seconds of birth in 8.5 out of 10 children. This is at a time when the babies are all covered in blood. Another study found that the presence of life is evidenced by the first breath, the activities of the blood begins to work towards helping other organs function:

> "Once the baby takes the first breath, a number of changes occur in the infant's lungs and circulatory system. Increased oxygen in the lungs causes a decrease in blood flow resistance to the lungs. Blood flow resistance of the baby's blood vessels also increases. Fluid drains or is absorbed from the respiratory system. The lungs inflate and begin working on their own, moving oxygen into the bloodstream and removing carbon dioxide by breathing out (U.S. National Library of Medicine)".

From the above studies, blood is a life-supplying component to every life. The Word of God in Ezekiel 16: 7 notes And when I passed by you and saw you struggling in your own blood, I said to you in your blood, 'Live!' Yes, I said to you in your blood, 'Live!'I made you thrive like a plant in the field; and you grew, matured, and became very beautiful. This is our reality in our first moments of life; life was given to us in the blood by the Word of God. Our blood yielded to the Word of God and received life.

The arrival of a child after pregnancy does not guarantee life, according to the Scriptures. This is why some children do not survive after the first few minutes of birth. Those of us privileged to make it did by the voice of God which roared "LIVE". Despite today's advancement in science, there is no medical professional that would guarantee you 100% of success with any blood procedure, not even for a simplified tooth extraction procedure; because the life of the animal is in the blood, and the exact location of life in the blood cannot be pinpointed as only the Lord God has the absolute power over the blood. This brings us into the realization that the gift of life was not as a result of the multivitamins or the best doctors who delivered us, but the mercy and voice of God which spoke forth "Live" while we struggled in the blood.

The Devils Fight Against the Blood of Babies

As seen above, there is so much that goes on after children are born. Also, because children come to the world free of sins, the devil is out to also use the blood of Jesus for sacrifice. For this reason, demonic agents gravitate towards places where children are being born because they seek to harvest the blood of innocent children for the devil. There are demonic agents who lurk around hospital labor rooms to harvest the lives of newborns for satanic transactions. This is why there is an entire industry focused on abortion and why there are so many abortion clinics around. Those who are shielded from these satanic operations are people who are shielded by the blood of Jesus and the Word of God.

PRAYERS FOR THE LIFE OF GOD'S POWER IN THE BLOOD

1. I confess that Jesus died for my sins and He has made me whole in the name of Jesus

2. The blood of Jesus is sufficient for me in the name of Jesus

3. Lord, cleanse away every work of pollution that is affecting my land negatively by the blood of Jesus.

4. My blood, hear the living Word of God, and receive the fullness of life found in the blood of Jesus.

5. Evil codes programmed into the sun, moon, star and the heavenlies against my blood, be wiped out by the blood of Jesus.

6. Evil ordinances written against my blood, are nullified by the blood of Jesus..

7. As long as God's covenant with the sun and moon

cannot be altered, my blood will not yield to any form of satanic manipulations in the name of Jesus.

8. Thou heavens, rise in support of God's covenant for my life in the name of Jesus

9. The Lord Jesus presides over my blood in the name of Jesus.

10. Lord Jesus, cover my body with your blood in the name of Jesus.

11. Blood of Jesus, infuse life into my blood in the name of Jesus

12. Thou sun, hear the Word of God, you shall not bring evil projection into my blood in the name of Jesus.

13. Thou moon, hear the word of God, you shall not bring illnesses into my blood in the name of Jesus.

14. Thou earth, hear the word of the Lord, you shall not bring curses upon my blood in the name of Jesus.

15. My blood is secured in the blood of Jesus.

16. My blood will not be shed on earth in the name of Jesus.

17. My blood will not yield to satanic manipulation.

18. My blood rejects evil pronouncement in the name of Jesus.

19. Thou sun, moon and star, you shall not accept evil projection into my life in the name of Jesus.

20. Covenants projecting evil into my blood, be annulled by the blood of Jesus.

21. Thou sun, moon and stars, when the enemy seeks to shed my blood, reject the shedding of my blood in the name of Jesus, but use the enemy's blood instead for it is written, the one who digs a pit shall fall into it.

22. Thou earth, do not open your mouth to receive my blood anytime the enemy seeks to shed my blood by the mercies in the blood of Jesus, but take my enemy's blood instead, in the name of Jesus, for it is written, the one who digs a pit shall fall into it.

23. Thou earth, reject every plans of the workers of iniquity to steal my blood, but bring the workers of iniquity into instant judgment in the name of Jesus

24. Thou earth, open up and swallow the council of darkness meeting to discuss the shedding of my blood in the name of Jesus.

25. Thou earth, let the blood of Jesus be sufficient for me, throughout my journey and assignment on earth in the name of Jesus.

NOTES

3

~

BLOOD CURRENCY

Years ago, a man who used to work with a wealthy politician with significant influence and power in an African country said, "I am very sorry for a lot of young ladies who date my boss because he usually sends people to sprinkle substances on the ground and tells his security guards to ensure his guests walk over the substances, then he has sexual relations with them".

Blood is being used as a currency for transacting and trading spiritual commodities, especially virtues. Any woman who gets into such sexual encounters opens their blood to the devil's use.

Types of Satanic Blood Transactions

The subject of satanic blood transaction is complex and defies logic. However, the story of the atonement of the blood of Jesus gives hope for understanding this subject. Before the blood of Jesus was shed, there was a constant need for the shedding of animal blood for sacrifice as written in Hebrews 9:13 *"For if the blood of bulls and goats and the ashes of a heifer, sprinkling the unclean, sanctifies for the purifying of the flesh"*. The Scripture noted the effectiveness of this method until the death of Jesus invalidated this method.

Also, there were other complex rituals needed including transferring iniquities of people to the head of animals as found below:

Aaron shall lay both his hands on the head of the live goat, confess over it all the iniquities of the children of Israel, and all their transgressions, concerning all their sins, putting them on the head of the goat, and shall send *it* away into the wilderness by the hand of a suitable man.

Leviticus 16:21 (NKJV)

The agents of darkness reject salvation, as a result, they still transact with blood. Just like the wealthy man who sprinkled demonic substances on the ground, there are still people walking in dark acts and transacting with blood and virtues of people. They do it for a number of reasons including:

1. Satanists look for people to take their place in judgment. They use others to stand as their replacement against the enemy's wrath

2. Satanists look for death replacements. If they are looking for someone to take his place in death, depending on the type of sacrifice, they infuse evil into people through satanic sexual exchanges

3. Satanists look to get wealthy by stealing the virtues of others.

This is one of the reasons why the Scripture lays down instructions on how to live life in faithfulness, gentleness, kindness based on the Word of God. When we follow these prescriptions, we avoid the afflictions of the enemy. When people go out of God's laid down instructions, they have unholy sexual alliances, lack of contentment and all sorts expose them to the use of darkness.

The Ordinance of Blood for Blood and Life for Life

One of the ordinances of God is what we call B*lood for Blood and Life for Life* as found in the book of Genesis 9:6 - "Whoever sheds man's blood, By man his blood shall be shed; For in the image of God He made man.

This ordinance states that whenever there is a sin, a repayment with life is required. Because the life of any living being is in the blood, the blood becomes the essential requirement for atoning for the sin. Hence, the blood is a spiritual currency for settling spiritual debts. As discussed in chapter 1, satanic agents are very familiar with blood transactions, they understand how to trade in the spirit realm using the payment of blood. This is why people who still live in darkness use the blood of goats, rams, pigs, birds and all sorts for sacrifice.

The Scripture below notes that the shedding of blood is compulsory for sins to be canceled.

And according to the law almost all things are purified with *blood*, and without shedding of *blood* there is no remission

Hebrews 9:22 NKJV

The ways of God have not changed from the beginning and will not change. The provision and commandment of God is that any soul that sins must die as stated in the Scripture below:

> Behold, all souls are Mine;
> The soul of the father
> As well as the soul of the son is Mine;
> The soul who sins shall die.
> **Ezekiel 18:4 NKJV**

However, there is a clause found in other parts of the Scripture concerning the same subject. The clause gives an exemption if there is a replacement that can stand in the place of the person that has committed the offense, the replacement must fulfill the death. This is why the Lord made a provision for blood as the object of atonement, replacing the sinner in the book of Leviticus 17:11 - *For the life of the flesh is in the blood, and I have given it to you upon the altar to make atonement for your souls; for it is the blood that makes atonement for the soul.*

Blood Money: A Search for Wealth with Blood

There are wealthy individuals who purchased their wealth with the blood of animals or even humans. This satanic act is a form of ritual called blood money. People who seek to obtain wealth through crooked means consult with satanic powers who demand for blood in exchange of wealth.

People usually think blood rituals occur by shedding blood, there are many ways: A lot of people participate in the blood money ritual without even knowing about it. The one who goes out on a date with a blood money ritualist to a fine restaurant and gets their meal paid for by their ritualist date is a participant in spending blood money. The lady whose ritualist boyfriend got an engagement ring for using blood money is a participant. People who enter into sexual activities are highly susceptible to blood money rituals. Problems have entered into people's lives as a result of these kinds of alliances.

Blood money rituals usually attract dire consequences. Those who perform blood sacrifices understand the consequences and know they are a timebomb waiting to explode. As a result, they usually seek to ruin many lives as soon as they can. This is why believers need to understand this subject and take advantage of the power in the blood of Jesus that gives freedom.

The Voice of Blood

The blood has a voice, and those who shed blood have a voice crying against them.

> And He said, "What have you done? The voice of your brother's blood cries out to Me from the ground. So now you *are* cursed from the earth, which has opened its mouth to receive your brother's blood from your hand. When you till the ground, it shall no longer yield its strength to you.
>
> **Genesis 4:10-12 NKJV**

The Scripture above noted that the voice of Abel cried from the ground to the Lord after Cain murdered him.

This is why Reuben advised his brothers to avoid shedding of the blood of Joseph:

> And Reuben said to them, "Shed no blood, *but* cast him into this pit which *is* in the wilderness, and do not lay a hand on him"—that he might deliver him out of their hands, and bring

him back to his father.

Genesis 37:22 NKJV

When the sin of bloodshed is in the life of an individual, the earth refuses to yield any blessings to sucd individuals because they have forced the land to participate in their abomination. Anywhere there is unrest, violence, blood crimes, there is hardly economic prosperity, because the land is under a curse of desolation as written in Ezekiel 7:23.

God takes blood crimes seriously and would not compromise. Past bloodshed can be the disqualifying factor for future breakthroughs. The chief priests who paid Judas to betray Jesus knew the consequences of blood crimes and responded *"But the chief priests took the silver pieces and said, "It is not lawful to put them into the treasury, because they are the price of blood."* Matthew 27:6. After getting paid to betray Jesus, he attempted to return the money to them but they refused because the money is associated with blood. A similar reason David was disqualified from building the house of God is explained in the Scripture below;.

"but the word of the Lord came to me, saying, you have shed much blood and have made great wars; you shall not build a house for My name, because you have shed much blood on the earth in my sight"
I Chronicles 22:8 (NKJV)

By the blood of Jesus, there is a way out; whether your virtues have been traded, or you have dabbled in satanic activities trading other people's destiny for satanic wealth, the only way out is Jesus. Jesus' blood is sufficient to pay all debts owed so that you don't pay it back with your blood.

PRAYERS OF DELIVERANCE FROM BLOOD RITUAL RELATED AFFILIATIONS

1. Lord Jesus, I confess that you are Lord over my soul in the name of Jesus

2. Father Lord, deliver me from every influences of satanic blood sacrifice in the name of Jesus

3. Father Lord, deliver my blood from the infusion of darkness in the name of Jesus

4. Enemies in my blood are cast out by the fire of the Lord in the name of Jesus.

5. Lord, remove all access that I have given to satan into my blood through unholy sexual alliances in the name of Jesus.

6. My blood will not be sacrificed on the altar of darkness in

the name of Jesus.

7. My blood is infused with the blood of Jesus.

8. My blood is covered with the blood of Jesus

9. The blood of Jesus shall overshadow my blood in the name of Jesus

10. My blood shall not be shed in the name of Jesus.

11. Lord deliver me from associations of ritualist in the name of Jesus

12. Father deliver me from the times I sponsored abortion in the name of Jesus

13. Father deliver me from the pangs of abortion in the name of Jesus

14. Father, deliver me from all sins of bloodshed in my ancestry in the name of Jesus

15. Blood of Jesus, cover my life in the name of Jesus.

16. My blood shall not be spent as a currency in the name of Jesus.

17. My blood rejects bewitchment in the name of Jesus.

18. Satanic blood ties are broken by the blood of Jesus.

19. Jesus, I release unto you, every ordinance and covenant that is written in the blood that is not your blood.

20. The blood of Jesus pays back all kinds of debt that the enemy is requiring of me, in the name of Jesus.

21. My blood is protected and under the covering of the blood of Jesus.

22. My life shall not be used as a ransom for rituals in the name of Jesus.

23. My blood shall not be accessible to the drinkers of blood, by the blood of Jesus.

24. My blood shall not be the drink of payback in the name of Jesus.

25. My blood shall not be traded in local markets and the foreign markets in the name of Jesus.

26. My blood shall not be taken into captivity in the name of Jesus.

27. My blood shall not be traded on the table of demons in the name of Jesus.

28. My blood is not available for sale in the name of Jesus.

29. My blood has been bought by the blood of Jesus.

30. The shedding of the blood of Jesus at Calvary is sufficient for my blood in the name of Jesus.

NOTES

4

~

BLOOD, ACCESS & TRANSFERS

Transfers take place through the blood, both good and bad. There was a pregnant lady whom we ministered to, and the Lord said to release a prayer over her: Pray against the flow of evil inheritance into the life of her baby. The Lord said there were major issues in her life she needed to pray out of her lineage, so the same patterns would not continue in her family. We did. She kept praying. During one of her tests, she realized that a lot of genes had been deleted from her baby on the blood test results handed over to her. Hallelujah! The blood carries both evil and good inheritance and as a result, the devil is interested in accessing the blood of individuals to introduce defilement.

Access into the Blood

Major life saving efforts involve access to the blood. Doctors draw blood to conduct tests or administer medication that needs to flow into the bloodstream. Sometimes, the only way a person may be revived is by blood transfusion. As medical professionals sometimes need access into the blood to save a person's life, access is also sought into people's life spiritually by the enemy. The fastest way for satanic agents to access people's lives and destiny is through blood contact. With access to a person's blood, satanic agents can study a person's life, and alter the cause of their lives.

Access into the Blood: Unholy Sexual Contacts

Any form of sexual intercourse gives access to the blood. When access is obtained into the blood especially through unholy sexual contacts, it is the highest form of defilement which brings such souls into nakedness and fitness as the presence of God departs such bodies. When the presence of God departs, access is opened to all forms of diseases, and all shapes of demons enter to afflict. Satanic transfers through sex brings complex spiritual problems which begins to manifests as, interwoven failure trends, deadlocks, atttraction to the wrong people or marriage, conflict in the mind, chronic confusion, mental retardation, multi-affliction stronghold. This is why sexual contact is usually the easiest way targeted by satanic agents to access people's blood.

Access into the Blood: Needles

The devil uses needles in a variety of ways to collect blood. Satanic hair stylists use needles while sewing hair extensions into people's hair and "mistakenly" poke the scalp to touch blood. The needles are submitted into covens afterwards. Access into the blood is obtained by satanic agents through the use of needles in a drug-abuse environment. Needles are being used to initiate people into the occult. Needles are used to pass demons into people. Needles are used to introduce infirmities into people.

Access into the Blood: Healthcare Environments

Also, in healthcare, needles are used to collect blood samples by demonic agents. Hence, God's children must be filled with prayers that their blood will not be harvested for demonic purposes. A few years ago, a nurse said, the hospital where she works usually has a high death rate and patients' conditions seem to get worse. She spoke out wondering what the problem was without knowing there were many satanic agents who were health care workers where she worked. Many of them introduce the worst demons into patients and sometimes doctors get confused as things turn out worse. In healthcare facilities, there are a lot of procedures requiring access to the blood, making it a high place of target for the devil to access blood. Many healthcare workers are in the occultic, and hold a lot of people captive spiritually in medical facilities, but the blood of Jesus prevails.

Access into the Blood through Family line

Satanic access can be easily obtained into a person's blood through their family lineage, grandparents, parents or siblings or by marriage. Access into the blood can be obtained by marriage. We ministered to a brother who was about getting married. The Lord said, tell him to fast for 3 days for God to open his eyes before he gets married to that woman who is about to import all sizes and shapes of poverty into his life and family. He did not listen, he went ahead with the marriage. Before marriage, the symptoms of poverty were already getting stronger, many people falling sick in the family and having to spend money in the hospital. The moment they got married, people within that family began to encounter job loss, and other situations threatening their finances. The only persons in such a family that will escape such battles are family members who diligently follow the instructions of the Holy Spirit and are filled with the power of the Holy Spirit.

Access into the Blood through Food

Food is another easy tool used by the enemy to access people's blood. Through food, people can send curses, demons and all sorts into people's blood. Through the use of food, agents of darkness reach into the blood of their unsuspecting victims. The Scripture calls it food sacrificed to idols in 1 Corinthians 10:28 - "But if anyone says to you, "This was offered to idols," do not eat it for the sake of the one who told you, and for conscience' sake; for "the earth *is* the LORD 's, and all its fullness."

Blood and Virtue Transfers

We ministered to an individual whose menstrual cycle was troubled, though she was not close to menopause. The Lord said, "she partook in an inheritance she was not supposed to partake into. Tell her to separate herself from that inheritance. Until she detaches herself from the inheritance of that family and focuses on chasing after the inheritance of the kingdom of God;

then, all that she has lost will come back". She said they just shared a family inheritance and she received some of it. These are deep spiritual mysteries that only the Lord understands. At first, when the Lord said that, we wondered what the relationship between an inheritance and the disappearance of a menstrual cycle was, but when she walked in obedience, there was restoration.

Open Sacrifices & Blood Exchanges

A man of God shared; one of his elders laid hands on him and ever since things went on a downward spiral for him in ministry and business. He did not know an open sacrifice had occurred. Open exchanges are common occurrences in the spiritual realm. Every time hands are laid on the head of a person and there is usually a spiritual transfer, either coming from the person laying hand on the other, or from the person being laid hands on. Only the very few people who carry the real power of God would lay hands and transfer the ordination of God into people's lives. Where there is no transfer of God's ordination, sin, defilement, pollution and problems are transfered. When the hands of a person whose soul is polluted is laid on another individual, this is called Open Sacrifice. They are making open sacrifices knowingly or unknowingly by transferring the pollution in their lives to the lives of others.

Before Jesus came, the ancient way of atoning for sins was to find a goat which the priest would lay his hands on to confess all his iniquities on. The Scripture below is being requoted:

Aaron shall lay both his hands on the head of the live goat, confess over it all the iniquities of the children of Israel, and all their transgressions, concerning all their sins, putting them on the head of the goat, and shall send *it* away into the wilderness by the hand of a suitable man.

Leviticus 16:21 NKJV

What Aaron was saying to the goat was, "goat, take my place and the place of the children of Israel in judgment". All the sins of the nation of Israel are then placed upon the goat.

Similarly, agents of darkness have mastered this concept and still put it into use today by transferring their sin. Every single time a hand is laid by agents of darkness, they say, "what I do not want in my life, I transfer it into this head".

The reality in spiritual transfer has not changed and this is why the Scripture in the new testament records:

Do not lay hands on anyone hastily,

nor share in other people's sins; keep yourself pure.

1 Timothy 5:22 (NKJV)

It is important for believers to know that the only reason why access is sought to the blood is to be able to transfer evil into the blood. However, the blood of Jesus has more power to shed off all evil in the blood just like it is written above in the story of the woman who was pregnant, and all evil in her blood was wiped out, so her child does not inherit.

PRAYERS OF WITHDRAWAL OF ACCESS INTO THE BLOOD GIVEN TO THE DEVIL

1. Lord, I surrender my life to you in the name of Jesus.

2. Lord Jesus, I withdraw all access given to witchcraft into my blood in the name of Jesus

3. Lord, close all the open doors satan is using as access into my blood, in the name of Jesus

4. Lord, close all the open doors through the wrong laying of hands that satan is using as access into my blood, in the name of Jesus

5. Lord, close all the open doors through past unholy sexual relations that satan is using as access into my blood, in the name of Jesus

6. Lord, close all the open doors of satanic food consumption that satan is using as access into my blood, in the name of Jesus

7. All access of the occultic into my blood is revoked by the blood of Jesus

8. All access of the wicked into my blood is revoked by the blood of Jesus

9. All access that I have willingly given to dark powers through sinful activities is revoked by the blood of Jesus in the name of Jesus

10. Blood of Jesus, be the shield over my life in the name of Jesus.

11. Blood of Jesus, be the protection overy my household in the name of Jesus

12. Blood of Jesus be the protection over the works of my hands in the name of Jesus

13. My blood, hear the word of God, do not harken to the commands of darkness in the name of Jesus

14. Access into my blood through satanic medical practitioners, be revoked by the blood of Jesus.

15. Blood of Jesus, visit every altar where my blood is being used for ritual, and remove my blood from such altars in the name of Jesus

16. Evil deposits by satanic sexual contacts in my blood, be flushed out by the blood of Jesus, in the name of Jesus.

17. Wherever my blood is being housed in satanic camps, Lord, let the blood of Jesus , set my blood free in the name of Jesus.

18. My blood is not for consumption by the power in the blood of Jesus.

19. My blood rejects satanic programmes for you in the name of Jesus.

20. Satanic access into my blood obtained through parental connection, blood of Jesus, revokes such access in the name of Jesus.

21. My blood shall not be used for rituals and sacrifice in the name of Jesus

22. My blood shall not be used to cleanse the land in the name of Jesus

23. My virtues cannot be stolen in the name of Jesus

24. Death has no place in my blood by the power in the blood of Jesus.

25. Father, cause a separation to occur and let my blood be withdrawn from all donation banks of witchcraft in the name of Jesus.

26. Father, as the waters were divided from the waters, let the blood of Jesus, separate my blood from the blood donated in the coven of witchcraft.

27. Father Lord, as the waters were divided from the waters in the beginning, let my blood be withdrawn from all satanic donation banks in the name of Jesus.

28. Lord Jesus, let my blood be withdrawn from all satanic covenants by your blood in the name of Jesus.

29. Lord Jesus, let my blood be delivered from every program of darkness in the name of Jesus.

30. My blood rejects bewitchment in the name of Jesus.

31. Representation of my blood taken to demonic covens, let the coven be shattered in the name of Jesus.

32. Demonic pronouncement into the origin of my blood to harm me, be nullified in the name of Jesus.

33. Powers mixed with my blood to afflict me is removed in the name of Jesus

34. Powers appearing in the spirit realm by my virtues of any blood as me to ruin my life are consumed by the fire of God, in the name of Jesus.

35. Missiles of darkness planted into my blood are expelled by the finger of God in the name of Jesus.

36. Demonic priest chanting death into my blood, is destroyed instead of me in the name of Jesus.

37. Cursed be anyone that curses my blood in the name of Jesus.

38. I plug my blood into heaven's power source in the name of Jesus.

39. The blood of Jesus flows within me, my blood refuses

manipulation.

40. The yoke of blood imbalance is broken in the name of Jesus.

NOTES

5

~

THE VOICE OF THE BLOOD

As briefly discussed in previous chapters, the blood has a voice, both the blood of man and of animals. The blood does speak. In this chapter, we discuss the ways in which blood speaks. Many ailments diagnoses are found through the blood. When doctors test for pregnancy, the gender of a baby or DNA, they use the blood for more accurate results.

All these tests simply mean that they are inquiring from the blood and the blood is giving responses. In these instances, the blood could say, "yes, there is a baby in this mother", and the test will come out as a positive pregnancy outcome. The blood could say, "no, there is no disease in this life", hence the blood result will test negative. For the pregnant mother carrying twins, the blood can speak about it in tests. For the child who has no knowledge of their father, the DNA test will say, "this is your real father". For those who have been sneaking to have ungodly sexual relations, their blood will give reports of their activities by saying, "their life has been infected with STDs". Science knows this and simply queries the blood through examination and tests. This is a wonderful mystery of God, placed in the blood.

The Bloodline Inheritance

Every covenant the Lord makes with a life is located in the blood. God's covenants are so powerful that it flows from one generation to the another through the blood line. Spiritually, the blood carries information about a person's life. Generational transfer of blessings or curses are carried through the blood. As couples have children, the children carry their parents' blood, and as they grow into adults and start their own family, the cycle repeats; and there are transfers by the blood. and sharing of inheritance by blood. Generational trends, patterns, history are preserved in the blood. Your parents may not leave your physical inheritance, but by blood, they left you a spiritual inheritance through the blood. This inheritance is what you need to figure out. When you ask, "God what kind of inheritance?" If you have been encountering problems, it is the blood speaking out saying "this is what is in me, this is what is in your blood line, this is what has been happening in the previous blood line".

Some people find out that wherever they go, everyone hates them, and they also find that happening to other people in their family. Some people find out that they get married late in their family. Some people find out that in their family line, they usually never bear a male child. Some people find out that it is rare for anyone to attain the age of 65 in their family line and most people die before their 65th year. Others find out that most people never get a college degree in their family. Others find out that after they get a college degree, they never obtain a good job or job at all. These are examples of blood inheritances. Some people are not actively involved in witchcraft groups, but they find out that they actively manipulate others even when they do not want to, this could be as a result of sharing the same bloodline with a mother who is a witch. Some people always attract the wrong men and women into their network, this can be a blood-inherited curse.

Believers must diligently study their bloodline to know what inheritances ame through their bloodline, and cast out evil inheritance, and work towards upholding the covenants of God in their blood.

The Call of Blood Vengeance

The voice of the blood can be the voice of vengeance. The call for blood vengeance occurs when the voice of a blood that

The Lord says those who shed blood shall have their blood shed. Jezebel manipulatively shed the blood of Naboth over his plot of land. When Jehu was made king, the meeting that would take Jezebel out took place on the same plot of land which Naboth was murdered for.

Now Jehu drew his bow with full strength and shot Jehoram between his arms; and the arrow came out at his heart, and he sank down in his chariot. Then *Jehu* said to Bidkar his captain, "Pick *him* up, *and* throw him into the tract of the field of Naboth the Jezreelite; for remember, when you and I were riding together behind Ahab his father, that the Lord laid this burden upon him: 'Surely I saw yesterday the blood of Naboth and the blood of his sons,' says the Lord, 'and I will repay you in this plot,' says the Lord. Now therefore, take *and* throw him on the plot *of ground,* according to the word of the Lord."

2 Kings 9:24-26

The Scripture records that the blood of Jezebel was shed on the same piece of land where Naboth's blood was shed;

Now when Jehu had come to Jezreel, Jezebel heard *of it;* and she put paint on her eyes and adorned her head, and looked through a window. Then, as Jehu entered the gate, she said, "*Is it* peace, Zimri, murderer of your master?" And he looked up at the window, and said, "Who *is* on my side? Who?" So two *or* three eunuchs looked out at him. Then he said, "Throw her down." So they threw her down, and *some* of her blood spattered on the wall and on the horses; and he trampled her underfoot. And when he had gone in, he ate and drank. Then he said, "Go now, see to this accursed *woman,* and bury her, for she was a king's daughter." So they went to bury her, but they found no more of her than the skull and the feet and the palms of *her* hands. Therefore they came back and told him. And he said, "This *is* the word of the Lord, which He spoke by His servant Elijah the Tishbite, saying, 'On the plot *of ground* at Jezreel dogs shall eat the flesh of Jezebel; and the corpse of Jezebel shall be as refuse on the surface of the field, in the plot at Jezreel, so that they shall not say, "Here *lies* Jezebel."

2 Kings 9:30-37 NKJV

Symptoms of the Call for Blood Vengeance

There is usually the call for blood vengeance upon people when they have committed the sins of abortion and other blood related sins. When there is a call for blood vengeance, there is the usually extreme hardship, and difficult to resolve issues, and sometimes prayers seem ineffective. Examples include hard financial distress, unresolvable problems, calamities, unending pains and much more.

PRAYERS TO SHIELD THE BLOOD FROM DEADLY BLOOD INHERITANCES

1. Father, let the voice of the blood of Jesus speak for me.
2. Lord Jesus, the powers of Jezebel has no hold over my blood in the name of Jesus
3. The powers of witchcraft have no claim over my blood in the name of Jesus.
4. Drinkers of blood and eaters of flesh, my blood and flesh is not your portion in the name of Jesus.
5. My blood is secured in the blood of Jesus.
    My blood will not be shed in the name of Jesus
6. Blood sucking demons, my blood is not your habitation because my blood has been mixed with the blood of Jesus.
7. Voice of death in my blood is silenced by the blood of Jesus.
8. My blood speaks life in the name of Jesus.
9. Covenant of death in my blood is annulled by the blood

of Jesus.

10. Blood of Jesus, cover my blood in the name of Jesus.

11. Inheritance of failure in my blood, be wiped out by the blood of Jesus

12. Inheritance of untimely death in my blood, is wiped out by the blood of Jesus

13. Inheritance of chronic poverty in my blood, is wiped out by the blood of Jesus

14. Inheritance of witchcraft in my blood, is wiped out by the blood of Jesus.

15. Inheritance of attracting wickedness in my blood, is wiped out by the blood of Jesus.

16. The blood of Jesus shall cancel all inheritance of affliction by bloodline, and give me life in the name of Jesus.

17. The blood of Jesus shall cancel all inheritance of wasters by bloodline from my life in the name of Jesus.

18. Lord, let your blessings deposited into my blood, begin to come alive by the blood of Jesus.

19. Blood of Jesus, speak power into my blood in the name of Jesus.

20. Blood of Jesus, protect my blood from all sorts of evil in the name of Jesus.

21. Voice of the Lord, speak over my blood in the name of

Jesus

22. Voice of the Lord, speak into my blood, and shatter and divide every fire of affliction planted into my blood in the name of Jesus.

23. The voice of the Lord that is over the water, speaks deliverance into my blood, in the name of Jesus.

24. The voice of the Lord shall scatter the cou

25. The voice of the Lord shall exposed the arrows of my blood,

26. Food of affliction mixed into my blood, be expelled by the blood of Jesus.

27. Demonic powers, shedding its own blood to invoke pity from evil powers, blood of Jesus, fight for me and deliver my blood.

28. Familiar powers, shedding its own blood to afflict my blood, blood of Jesus, speak for me in the name.

29. Inheritance of death in my blood, get out of my blood, by the blood of Jesus.

30. Every demonic seed of darkness into my blood is uprooted in the name of Jesus.

31. Irregular blood flow is healed in the name of Jesus.

32. Demon of odor in the blood, get out of my blood in the name of Jesus.

33. Activities of demonic at intervals in my blood are expelled by the finger of God, in the name of Jesus.

34. Evil fellowship in my blood is cast out in the name of Jesus.

35. Lord Jesus, let Your blood be the only blood that is mixed with my blood, in the name of Jesus.

NOTES

6

~

BATTLES OF THE BLOODLINE

The hardest kinds of war to overcome in the spirit realm are the bloodline blood. They are called battles of the blood; These are battles originating from people who are tied by blood. These battles are difficult to uncover, and lay claim to the power and legal covenants in the blood. To understand this concept, we discuss bloodline relationships in the next segment.

Bloodline & Blood Tie

Bloodline and blood ties are not used interchangeably in this book, as a result, we discuss their differences here. The bloodline is the lineage from which a person originates. Blood ties are bonds and contract formed between the blood of two or more people as result of marriage, sex, covenants or contact through blood.

Levels of the Bloodline Relationships

There are different levels of bloodline. The level of bloodline is the degree of closeness one person has to another by blood. There are two levels of bloodline relationship:

Natural Bloodline Relationship: These are blood relationships existing by no design of the parties involved but by the Lord. We do not get to choose our siblings, we do not get to choose our parents. Natural bloodline relationships include relationships between parents and children, relationships between siblings.

Legalized Bloodline Relationship: These are blood relationships which were formed as a result of marriage, or sexual relationships with others. There are godly legalized bloodline relationships which is the relationship formed between husband and wife. Also, there are satanically legalized bloodline relationships which occurred as a result of unholy sexual relationships between individuals.

Blood Ties

Blood ties are covenants binding the blood of two or more people together. Blood ties exist when two or more people make a covenant and the covenant is sealed with the blood.

There are good blood ties, and also the evil ones. We look at the instances of blood ties below:

Evil Blood Ties

Unholy Sexual Relations: Blood ties can exist between a man and a woman who had sex together outside of matrimony.

Blood Exchange by Objects: Blood ties can be formed when two people share the same razor, or when two blood has been put together, two lives are joined together, and people begin to experience similar occurrences.

Evil Covenants: Blood ties are shared when people make covenants by blood or swear by blood.

Eating/Drinking of Blood: Blood ties can be formed when

people consume meat containing blood. Deuteronomy 12:23 warns "Only be sure that you do not eat the *blood*, for the *blood* is the life; you may not eat the life with the meat".

The major issue with blood ties related battles is that people who share blood ties encounter the same problems such as diseases, marital problems, poverty because there is a strong tie in the blood.

Division of the Blood

Division of the blood occurs when the blood ties between two people with natural strong blood ties form stronger blood ties with others. For example; a child who had a strong blood tie with the parent matures and gets married and forms their own family. The natural blood tie between the parent and child still exists, but a new legalized and more powerful blood tie is formed with the spouse. In Genesis 2:24, the Scriptures note, "Therefore a man shall leave his father and mother and be joined to his wife, and they shall become one flesh". This concept is called the division of the blood. The division of the blood usually occurs for the branching out and multiplication of God's covenant in an upcoming generation.

Types of Bloodline Wars

Bloodline wars are battles fighting you from a source which is tied to you by blood. They are potent, powerful, battles with legal footholds. These battle types are the most difficult to detect, and even more hard to defeat. Below are the most common types of blood wars.

Spousal Blood War: The Scripture below speaks concerning spouses who have entered into satanic partnership with the devil, and their object of sacrifice is their spouse. We met a woman and the Lord said to her, " You go to church and hide under the name of Jesus, yet you go to your satanic coven at nights bringing your husband's name for affliction and tying your family down". The husband could not get a job, their young teenages were toying with night life and the family was tearing apart, yet the Lord was calling the wife into repentance because she had entered into witchcraft covenants. For blood battles like this, if undetected and unresolved, the family would remain in bondage because the one who is afflicting them is one of their blood, with a legal covenant of marriage.

Parental Blood War: During a worship session in 2016, the Lord released a Word; "There is a woman here, and you have gone to tie that child's life somewhere, if you do not release the life of that child and repent, the Lord will fight for the child and this is what will happen to you...". After the service, a woman came forward, she said *was very scared because God said the person who has held the child's life will pay back with their life.* So we asked her, are you the one holding any child's life down? She began her story and how they gave her some satanic object to afflict others.

The utmost kind of warfare that defeats people most is one from enemies who are blood relations, these are called blood wars. Before the Lord spoke about the blood in Ezekiel 16, he spoke about the background of Jerusalem, He says, "this is where you came from, you came from a wicked background". Your navel cord ties you to your other in the womb. It does not mean that because you passed through a family line, that the family line would be friendly towards your destiny. God told Abraham to leave his father's house because the place was not favorable towards destiny. Many people with great purposes are born into wickedness. These kinds of wars seek to bring the satanic prophecy "like mother like daughter".

The Scripture below speaks about parents who have

entered into satanic partnership with the devil, and their object of sacrifice is their children.

Jeremiah 19:5

(they have also built the high places of Baal, to burn their sons with fire *for* burnt offerings to Baal, which I did not command or speak, nor did it come into My mind),

Many children have died young without no one knowing the cause of their death, when the case is such that one or both of their parents are satanists, and are the ones who used them for blood sacrifices. There are some situations where children develop chronic illnesses, or become imbeciles, crippled, or experiencing major organ failure, and doctors cannot pinpoint what is wrong, or doctors even find problems. Children who are held captives under these kinds of battles cannot be lukewarm Christians, like those who go to church just to socialize without carrying God's power, otherwise, they will be wasted by the emptiers of life.

Parents who enter into witchcraft covenants are usually

required to sacrifice the people they hold most dear to them, usually their spouse and their children. This is why when people go through this kind of blood war, it is usually a win or die war because they share the blood of the people fighting them within them. The way forward is to enter your life in totality into God's power and pray hard to be able to come out triumphantly and unhurt.

Child-to-Parent War: There are some children who have been initiated into witchcraft, and the parents have no idea. Such children bring all sorts of troubles into the family, they may bring in the spirit of chronic poverty, illnesses just to ensure their parents have no rest. It gets worse when the family attends a church where the Holy Spirit is not present. If care is not taken, such children will ensure the affliction of the parents. If your child is the one bringing you affliction, there is a battle in your blood you should fight. You will need to seek God's deliverance by the power of the Holy Spirit and the Lord will deliver this child.

Incisions/Tattoos: Incisions also start blood wars. People are told that if they make incisions on their body, there will be protection; these are some of the ways the devil has lured people into satanic groups. The recipe from incisions and tattoos are obtained from the depths of the pit of hell and carries along demons and goes straight into the blood. The problem with this kind of battle is that it is a potent weapon the enemy uses to fight many as they legally open up their blood to the devil. This is one of the reasons why the Lord forbids tattoo in Leviticus 19:28 where the Lord declares it an abomination to make cuts in the body.

Covenants: When people go to make covenants with others, cutting their wrists and exchanging words over their blood, there is already a battle in the blood. This satanic practice has long been carried on between friends, sexul partners and business partners where they promise one another not to betray. If you have been involved in this, there is a raging battle in your blood you need to fight now.

Blood-Related Profession: Believers who work in the healthcare field need to be charged by the fire of the Holy Spirit. Alot of afflictions and family division occurs in the lives of many healthcare professionals because they are exposed to a lot of blood with a lot of activities ongoing. We ministered to a lot of immigrant families who entered into the healthcare profession in

America, especially nursing. One trend was that families were breaking apart and the spirits of violence, anger, drunkenness, jealousy, promiscuity crept into these families. Many of these are not of natural causes, but these are manifestations of demons within the blood. These are a replay of the happenings in the blood of the people they care for; and many families get torn apart as a result. Believers in healthcare need to overcome these satanic forces by the power in the blood of Jesus.

PRAYERS TO DEFEAT BLOODLINE BATTLES

1. By the resurrection power of Jesus, I shall not be defeated by bloodline battles in the name of Jesus.

2. Lord, uproot wickedness from my blood in the name of Jesus

3. Let the blood of Jesus break every satanic deposit formed in my blood in the name of Jesus.

4. Blood of Jesus, visit the blood of my spouse and purify in the name of Jesus

5. Blood of Jesus, visit the blood of my children and purify in the name of Jesus.

6. Blood of Jesus, break every all satanic blood ties that I am a part of in the name of Jesus

7. By the power in the blood of Jesus, I overcome the transference of demons by blood in the name of Jesus Blood of Jesus, visit my foundation in the name of Jesus.

8. Blood of wickedness in my blood, be purged out by the

blood of Jesus

9. Blood of witches in my blood, be flushed out by the blood of Jesus

10. Blood of Jesus, flush out every demon of affliction in my blood

11. Blood of Jesus, expel poverty from my blood in the name of Jesus.

12. Blood of Jesus, expel folly from my blood in the name of Jesus

13. Blood of Jesus, deliver my blood for transgenerational affliction in the name of Jesus.

14. Blood of Jesus, overshadow my blood in the name of Jesus

15. Blood of Jesus, cleanse my blood in the name of Jesus.

16. Demons fighting me from within my blood, be cast out by the blood of Jesus.

17. I drink the blood of Jesus, therefore, all poisons in my blood are flushed out in the name of Jesus.

18. I hand over my life to the care of the blood of Jesus.

19. Food of affliction mixed into my blood, be expelled by the blood of Jesus.

20. Demonic powers, shedding its own blood to invoke pity from evil powers, blood of Jesus, fight for me and deliver

my blood.

21. Familiar powers, shedding its own blood to afflict my blood, blood of Jesus, speak for me in the name.

22. Familiar blood, donating my blood into demonic blood banks, let the blood of Jesus speak deliverance my blood, in the name of Jesus.

23. Demonic operation of the enemy to harvest my blood, be destroyed in the name of Jesus.

24. Seed in my blood attracting death, you are uprooted in the name of Jesus.

25. I break the yoke of the aggressive enemy of my blood, in the name of Jesus.

26. Monitoring devices in my blood, monitoring my blood for evil, be destroyed by the fire of the Holy spirit.

27. Sickness of the destroyer in my blood, in the name of Jesus.

28. Foreign powers residing in my blood are hereby cast out in the name of Jesus.

29. Powers deceiving me from within my blood is cast out in the name of Jesus.

30. Intrusion of darkness in my blood is flushed out in the name of Jesus

31. Powers eating me up from within my blood is flushed out

by the blood of Jesus

32. Heavenly Physician, visit all parts of my blood in the name of Jesus.

33. Heavenly Physician, visit the foundation of my blood in the name of Jesus.

34. Holy Ghost fire, send your fire into my blood for purification.

NOTES

7

~

THE BLOOD OF JESUS

The power and the use of the blood of Jesus is still less understood today. The previous chapters discussed a lot about the blood. In this chapter we discuss the blood of Jesus.

The blood of Jesus is a multi-dimensional wonder. It carries different powers including; the powers of salvation, atonmentment, redemption, healing, revelational, substitution, cleansing, protective and the list is endless.

God's ordinance states that there must be an atonement for all sins; this ordinance still holds till date. In the times past, the blood of goats and bulls has been used in exchange for the blood that sinned, but that old method has been annulled.

Many believers are still held in captivity by false priests because they are yet to harness the power in the blood of Jesus.

People are still told to go buy chickens, goats and cows for sacrifice. These satanic rituals bring complications into people's lives, and everyone who conducts them does as a result of ignorance.

The Need for the Power in the Blood of Jesus

The blood of Jesus is all that we need to tackle tough and strange spiritual problems. Due to the complexities of this world, people encounter strange wars under heaven. A mother tries to have a child, she goes through excruciating pain and afterwards the devil wants to take the life of the child through sickness or any other way. The Scripture says in Revelation 12:11, "And they overcame him by *the blood of the Lamb*, and by *the* word *of* their testimony; and they loved not their lives unto death" . The book of Job mentions that a stillbirth is better than a person who does not fulfill their purpose. This Scripture teaches that when we have life, there is no excuse for failure especially because of the availability of the blood of Jesus.. After salvation, there is a purpose to fulfill, to fulfill that purpose, the knowledge of the blood of Jesus must be opened to the believer to live victoriously.

Believers, new or old, should ask the question;. "What is the blood of Jesus? How much do I know about the blood of Jesus? How effective is the blood of Jesus? What does the blood of Jesus do for me? When you begin to ask these questions, then the Lord begins to release knowledge in this area. The blood of Jesus carries major powers in 7 functional areas. See below:

#1 Atonement Powers: The primary function of the blood of Jesus is repayment of sins. The blood of Jesus works for atonement. For all the sins of the world, yours, parents', environmental sins, community sins that may be upon the believer, the blood of Jesus was shed to make atonement for it all. Regardless of how much riches people have, money is not the currency for atonement of sins. Satanists use blood of animals or even human animals for atonement sacrifices but there is a limitation and expiry date to that, and also, the use of the blood of animals has been invalidated after Jesus' blood was shed. This is the grace we enjoy as believers, the blood of Jesus offers atonement for our sins, as written below;

knowing that you were not redeemed with corruptible things, *like* silver or gold, from your aimless conduct *received* by tradition from your fathers, but with the precious blood of Christ, as of a lamb without blemish and without spot

1 Peter 1:18-19 NKJV

With the power of atonement in the blood of Jesus, cancellation of sin occurs.

#2 The Blessing of Life: The power of life is given to the believer through the flesh and blood of Jesus through the Holy Communion. The blood of Jesus was poured out as burnt offerings for our sins, and instead of death, we receive the abundance supply of life.

The cup of blessing which we bless, is it not the communion of the blood of Christ? The bread which we break, is it not the communion of the body of Christ?

1 Corinthians 10:16 NKJV

#3 Substitution: The blood of Jesus stands as a substitution for our blood. God's ordinance of substitution allows for the blood of Jesus to become a substitute for our blood. When demonic agents commit an abomination, the devil ensures they pay back, or they look for a substitution. There is a higher blood that believers can claim and work in, it is the substituting power in the blood of Jesus.

#4 Power of Access:

The blood of Jesus carries powers that give access into the glorious presence of God. If not for the blood of Jesus, we would not be able to approach God in worship and prayers. The blood of Jesus washes us and purifies us, making us admissible into God's presence.

Hebrews 10:19 NKJV

Having therefore, brethren, boldness to enter into the holiest by the blood of Jesus

Ephesians 2:13 NKJV

But now in Christ Jesus you who once were far off have been brought near by the blood of Christ

#5 Power for Negotiation:

Where blood sins are presence, nakedness and desolation set in. This is when people's protection departs, health fails, resources are insufficient, and blood sucking demons kick into action. When there is a voice of revenge crying against a person demanding judgment, the voice of the blood of Jesus silences such cries and mercy is released. The blood of Jesus negotiates on behalf of the believer for better contracts. The blood of Jesus does not allow the believer to be relegated into a life of punishment and hardship, but speaks life, greatness and power, thereby repositioning the believer for the best inheritance.

Hebrews 12:24 NKJV

"to Jesus the Mediator of the new covenant, and to the blood sprinkling that speaks better things than that of Abel.

#6 Cleansing Powers

Sin is filthy in God's sight. One of the powers in the blood of Jesus is the cleansing power in the blood. The blood of Jesus cleanses the sinners from the filthiness of sin. The blood of Jesus cleanses the former prostitute, the former adulterer, the former thief, the former murderer, the former rapist and transforms them into a new creation who is being used for God's glory.

Hebrew 9:14 NKJV

How much more shall the blood of Christ, who through the eternal Spirit offered HImself without spot to God, cleanse your conscience from dead works to serve the living God?

Revelation 1:5 NKJV

and from Jesus Christ, the faithful witness, the firstborn from the dead, and the ruler over the kings of the earth. To

#7 Universal Power

In the old testament, the kind of sin determines the kind of blood sacrifice required. This is why there is the burnt offering, grain offering, fellowship offering, sin offering and all forms of offering. Those who conduct satanic sacrifices today know that each sacrifice requires a unique payment. The blood of Jesus is without limitation, valid and works for everyone, for all types of sins across all regions, regardless of the situation.

Revelation 5:9 ERV

And they sang "a new song, saying,"Worthy are you to take the

scroll and to open its seals, for you were slain, and by your

blood you ransomed people for God

from every tribe and language and people and nation

#8 Revelatory Power

In the same verse, the Scripture reveals that the blood of Jesus counted Him worthy as the only one who was found worthy in heaven to open a sealed scroll to have access to the content of the scroll.

Revelation 5:9 ERV

And they sang "a new song, saying,"Worthy are you to take the

scroll and to open its seals, for you were slain, and by your

blood you ransomed people for God

from every tribe and language and people and nation

Revelatory gifts are hidden in the blood of Jesus, and anyone who enters into the blood of Jesus will be gifted with the spirit of God's revelation, which is the power of the Holy Spirit. This is why Jesus said the Lord will send the Promise. The Holy Spirit came after the blood of Jesus had been shed. Only a very few, who were prophets, had access to the Holy Spirit before Jesus came.

#9 Resurrection Power

Since life is in the blood, and by sin death has entered into the blood of all, Jesus came to give life back through His blood. Hence, His blood brings resurrection. When the blood of Jesus is applied to dead situations, life comes back. In resurrection there is healing. When the blood of Jesus is applied on curses, curses disappear and healing happens. This is only available through the blood of Jesus.

#10 Healing Power

The blood of Jesus carries the power of healing. When the blood of Jesus is applied to dead organs, life comes back. One of the testimonies we received during the February 2020 Worship unto deliverance is that the Holy Spirit led us through a Worship by the blood session where the Lord fed us with word on the blood and worship through songs of the blood of Jesus. A prophecy was released during the worship, "there is someone here, God is working on your menstrual cycle". After the worship, a woman testified that right there on that night, her menstrual cycle came forth. Halleluyah. When people are in deadly situations, and they apply the blood of Jesus, it works wonders just as healing was received by the woman who had blood flow for 12 years when she touched the garment of Jesus.

PRAYERS OF DELIVERANCE BY THE POWER IN THE BLOOD OF JESUS

1. Lord Jesus, let the power in your blood speak for me today in the name of Jesus

2. Father, let the life in the blood of Jesus be made whole in me in the name of Jesus

3. Blood of Jesus, speak power into my blood in the name of Jesus

4. Every catastrophe transported into my blood, blood of Jesus, shed it off in the name of Jesus.

5. Catastrophe fired into my bloodstream is destroyed by the nullifying power of the blood of Jesus.

6. Every bloodline demon assigned to my blood, your time is up, perish in the name of Jesus.

7. Blood of Jesus be infused with my bloodstream and flush

out every blockage

8. Blood of Jesus be infused with my bloodstream and flush out every infirmity

9. Blood of Jesus be infused with my bloodstream and flush out every deposit of darkness

10. Blood of Jesus be infused with my bloodstream and flush out every evil that my blood will become as pure to the blood of Jesus

11. I appropriate the blood of Jesus that was shed at Calvary upon my life

12. Blood of Jesus, wash me clean from every satanic laying of hands in the name of Jesus.

13. Satanic payload placed upon my by the demonic of hands, blood of Jesus shed it off in the name of Jesus

14. I testify to the blood of Jesus, therefore make available to me the fullness of God's power embedded in the blood of Jesus

15. I prophesy and pour the blood of Jesus into my future in the name of Jesus

16. My life is under the management of the blood of Jesus.

17. Lord, cover me where I am spiritually naked with the blood of Jesus.

18. Lord, cover me where I am mentally naked with the

blood of Jesus.

19. Lord, cover me where I am financially naked with the blood of Jesus.

20. Lord, cover me where I am emotionally naked with the blood of Jesus.

21. Let the blood of Jesus cleanse the effects of the blood of goats or other demonic blood sacrifices that I have been a part of in the name of Jesus.

22. Reveal unto me the power in the blood of Jesus

23. O God my father, make available unto me the power in the blood of Jesus.

24. Healing power in the blood the Lord, be made available unto me in the name of Jesus.

25. Redemption power in the blood of Jesus, redeem me in the name of Jesus

26. Blood of Jesus, cleanse my life from all forms of dirt in the name of Jesus

27. Blood of Jesus, cleanse all my organs from all diseases in the name of Jesus

28. Blood of Jesus, multiply life unto me in the name of Jesus

29. Blood of Jesus, cover me on all sides in the name of Jesus

30. Blood of Jesus, mediate on my behalf in the name of Jesus

31. Blood of Jesus, open unto me deep and secret things in the name of Jesus

32. Blood of Jesus, resurrect every good thing that is dead back to life in the name of Jesus.

33. Blood of Jesus, give men for my sake in the name of Jesus

34. Blood of Jesus, make available life unto me in the name of Jesus

35. Blood of Jesus speaks for me in place of judgment in the name of Jesus

36. Blood of Jesus flows into my mind in the name of Jesus.

NOTES

BIBLIOGRAPHY

Patel, Archana, et al. "Comparison of Perinatal Outcomes in Facilities before and After Global Network's Helping Babies Breathe Implementation Study in Nagpur, India." *BMC Pregnancy and Childbirth* 19 (2019)*ProQuest*. Web. 29 Feb. 2020.

U.S. National Library of Medicine, Changes in the newborn at birth https://medlineplus.gov/ency/article/002395.htm

ABOUT THE AUTHORS

Ebenezer Gabriels is a Worshipper, Innovation Leader, Prophetic Intercessor, and a Computer Scientist who has brought heaven's solutions into Financial markets, Technology, Government with his computational gifts. Prophet Gabriels is anointed as a Prophetic Leader of nations with the mantle of healing, worship music, national deliverance, foundational deliverance, complex problem-solving and building Yahweh's worship altars.

Abigail Ebenezer-Gabriels is Pastor, Teacher, Worshipper and a Multi-disciplinary leader in Business, Technology, Education and Development. She is blessed with prophetic teaching abilities with the anointing to unveil the mysteries in the Word of God. She is a Multi-specialty Speaker, with a special anointing to explain Heaven's ordinances on earth.

Both Ebenezer Gabriels and Abigail Ebenezer-Gabriels are the founders of the Ebenezer Gabriels Schools of the Holy Spirit and are the Senior Pastors of LightHill Church Gaithersburg, Maryland.

They lead several worship communities including the 6-Hour Worship Unto Deliverance, Innovation Lab Worship encounters, Move this Cloud - and prophetic podcast communities including the *Daily Prophetic Insight*s and *Prophetic Fire* where God's agenda for each day is announced and the manifold wisdom of God is revealed on earth.

Both Ebenezer Gabriels and his wife, Abigail Ebnezer-Gabriels joyfully serve the Lord through lifestyles of worship and their mandate is to build worship altars to intercede for nations.

Other Books by Ebenezer and Abigail Gabriels

Worship

Worship is Expensive

War of Altars

Business and Purpose

Unprofaned Purpose

Marriage

Heaven's Gate way to a Blissful marriage for Him

Heaven's Gateway to a Blissful marriage for Her

Deliverance from the Yokes of Marital Ignorance

Pulling Down the Strongholds of Evil Participants in Marriage

Prophetic

Activating Your Prophetic Senses

Dreams and Divine Interpretations

Family Deliverance

Uncursed

Deliverance from the Yoke of Accursed Names

Deliverance from the Curse of Vashti

Deliverance from the Yoke of Incest

Deliverance from the Wrong Family Tree

Mind

Deliverance from the Yokes Deep Mysteries of Creation in the Realms of Thoughts, Imaginations and Words

Spiritual War and Prayers

Rapid Fire

The Big Process called Yoke

Deliverance of the Snares of the Fowler

The only Fire that Extinguishes Witchcraft

No longer Fugitives of the Earth

Subduers of the Earth

Prayers of the Decade

Growth and Advancing in Faith

Deeper Mysteries of the Soul (English, Spanish, Arabic and Chinese)

Men: Called out of the Dunghill

Women: Bearers of Faith

New Beginnings in Christ

Wisdom my Companion

Deeper Mysteries of the Blood

Nations and intercessions

The Scroll and the Seal

America: The Past, the Present and the Next Chapter

Herod: The Church and Nigeria

Prophetic Insights into the Year

21 Weapons of Survival for 2021

2022 Meet the God Who Saves Blesses Shepherds and Carries

**Ebenezer
Gabriels**
ministries

At Ebenezer Gabriels Ministries (EGM), we fulfill the mandate of building worship altars by sharing the story of the most expensive worship ever offered by Jesus Christ, the Son of God and dispersing the aroma of the knowledge of Jesus Christ to the ends of the world.

Ebenezer Gabriels Publishing delivers biblically-grounded learning experiences that prepare audiences for launch into their prophetic calling. We create educational contents and deliver in innovative ways through online classrooms, apps, audio, prints to enhance the experience of each audience as they are filled with the aroma of Christ knowledge and thrive in their worship journey.

EGM currently operates out of Gaithersburg in Maryland, USA.

CONTACT

Office/Mailing
19644 Club House Road Suite 815, Gaithersburg, Maryland,
20876 USA

hello@ebenezergabriels.org
www.ebenezergabriels.org

OTHER BOOKS BY EBENEZER & ABIGAIL GABRIELS

Updated
Edition

DEEPER MYSTERIES
OF THE
SOUL

Ebenezer Gabriels
Abigail Ebenezer-Gabriels

RAPID FIRE

Apostolic prayers that evoke heaven's swift
response to major spiritual attacks.

New Edition

Ebenezer Gabriels
Abigail Gabriels

UNCURSED

A PROPHETIC BOOK TO RAISE A CURSELESS GENERATION

Features
BACK-TO-THE-Womb
deliverance prayers

Prayers before, during &
after pregnancy

Prayers for babies in the
womb
And more

Ebenezer Gabriels
Abigail Gabriels

The ONLY
FIRE
that extinguishes witchcraft

Prayers
Included

Ebenezer Gabriels
Abigail Gabriels

SUBDUERS
of the Earth

Ebenezer Gabriels
Abigail Gabriels

DEEPER MYSTERIES

OF THE

SOUL

Ebenezer Gabriels
Abigail Gabriels

Made in United States
North Haven, CT
16 July 2023